I AM SPARTACUS

WE ARE ALL GLADIATORS IN OUR CHOSEN FIELDS OF ENDEAVOR

WS BOYKIN

authorHOUSE®

AuthorHouse™
1663 Liberty Drive
Bloomington, IN 47403
www.authorhouse.com
Phone: 1 (800) 839-8640

Published by AuthorHouse 02/10/2016

ISBN: 978-1-5049-7774-6 (sc)
ISBN: 978-1-5049-7775-3 (e)

Library of Congress Control Number: 2016901811

Print information available on the last page.

Any people depicted in stock imagery provided by Thinkstock are models, and such images are being used for illustrative purposes only. Certain stock imagery © Thinkstock.

This book is printed on acid-free paper.

Because of the dynamic nature of the Internet, any web addresses or links contained in this book may have changed since publication and may no longer be valid. The views expressed in this work are solely those of the author and do not necessarily reflect the views of the publisher, and the publisher hereby disclaims any responsibility for them.

FOREWORD

David Mason

When Bill asked me to do this I was taken back a bit, but since I have known Bill for some 20 years from our first meeting in Squaw Valley for a 49ers event, to trips together in Napa Valley, to his home in the Bay area and in Nashville, to even allowing Bill on my tour bus for a short 3 gig stint. One thing I am sure of is his persistence like mine, is relentless. Like myself his life is spent on the road, which in itself takes a certain mind set. I have seen how he prepared for not only issues pertaining to the San Francisco 49er Foundation, (who hired me 3 times to perform at affairs), but also in his business dealings, both in the wine industry and more recently in the spirits business, his company had one of their brands prominently displayed on my tour bus for rolling advertising. Just as I need to fine tune my craft with constant playing of the guitar, and keeping a pad and paper close by for that next song idea, the principles of preparation and persistence and certainly team building, all apply to both of our life's journey.

Randall "Randy" Laureat Cross, Professional Football analyst, professional Football player, 6 time all-pro & 3 time Super Bowl Champion with the San Francisco 49ers and a 2 time All-American at UCLA and a 2011 College Football Hall of Fame member.

Bill has asked if I might write a foreword that encapsulated how this booklet/book and its key points applied to my life's journey. As a professional athlete, I had a foundation built from high school, through my years at UCLA in terms of strength training that continued all through my years in the NFL. The bigger aspect I see throughout the book is a reference to Goal setting and TEAM. During my tenure with the 49ers and to the same point with the great UCLA teams we set a finite Goal in the beginning of every season. In college that was to win our conference and go to the Rose Bowl. In my senior season we did that and beat #1 Ohio State. As a professional we did the same Goal setting with the Super Bowl and Lombardi trophy as our only acceptable goal. We went there 3 times during my playing days and won all three times. Persistence, Perseverance, Goal Setting, staying healthy are all points in this book that were so true in the results we achieved as a team and that I was fortunate enough to achieve as both an All-American and All-Pro from an individual point of view. During my off-seasons in the NFL I worked in a wide variety of areas, sales for a Medical Malpractice company, I owned a Silver, Gold & precious metals recovery company for several years and co-founded a Promotions & Advertising agency, all while I was an active player. Persistence & Follow thru are at the core of every endeavor I've ever been associated with on or off the playing field. One would do well to read + absorb these lessons. The title "I am Spartacus" has every application available to either the professional athlete or businessman.

The exact day we met will most likely never be known, but Bill and I agree, it was in a high school golf match at a public "dirt track" on the east side of Atlanta GA, an old 1920's design named Forest Hills GC, only a few miles from the famed East Lake Golf Club. There was something about Bill that struck me from the time I met him; his joy for life, his hilarious sense of humor, his intensity and competitive nature, but perhaps most importantly, there was a boldness about him, that as a much quieter, more reflective soul, I loved! I felt more confident around him and I wanted more of that charisma in my own life and now, over 40 years later, our friendship burns as brightly today as it did when we were 16 year old "striplings" learning our way through life together. A testimony to friendship, faith and respect!

As roommates throughout our four years of college, work-mates at *Barons*, a high end retail men's clothing store in Atlanta, travel-mates on the national junior and amateur circuits, and now his "Club Professional" at Secession Golf Club, where he has been a member since 1990, "Boink", as I affectionately call him, has remained one of those dear friendships that has endured since our high school days. In most people's lives, there are usually only two or three that stay together that long. After college we went our own ways, Bill to the business world, where his successes began to pile up, mostly on the west coast of CA and his long association as a VP of Seagrams Wine. I on the other hand went into the world of professional golf and after 8 years as a full time player and a short stint on the PGA Tour, I decided I could not live without the game of golf in my life on a daily basis, and I began my PGA apprenticeship in the Low Country of SC, Hilton Head Island to be exact. After many years of physical separation, never complete separation for we always stayed in touch, Bill and I were once again reunited by the common ground of Secession Golf Club and now this wonderful club affords us the opportunity to see each other on a regular basis.

As Bill undertook the effort you now hold in your hand, *I Am Spartacus*, he asked and I was honored to write a foreword in support of what Bill knows best, the art of the sale. As documented earlier, from our earliest days together, there was something about "Boink" that set him apart from so many others that I met in the game of golf. I truly believe it was the "salesman" within him, the confident, brash swagger of a man who could not be stopped. Failure never stopped him, success only pushed him harder and it was his inner confidence that has made him the success he now enjoys today. All I know about Bill and the one constant I've always used when describing him is, "That man can sell snow to the Eskimos!" Now, for the first time, his methods behind this success are revealed within the pages of *I Am Spartacus a*nd I know that you will enjoy this read as much as Bill has enjoyed bringing it to you. From a look deep inside corporate structures, to the profile of great executives and athletes, success has a common strain and Bill will bring all to light in this great read.

Enjoy it and may this great new book bring you to a higher level of success!

Michael S. Harmon, PGA
Director of Golf
Secession Golf Club
Beaufort, SC USA

William Roger Clemens, "The Rocket", 11 time all -star, 7 Cy Young Awards, 1 League MVP and 2 World Series Championships.

Bill asked if I might write a foreword encompassing any part of the subjects he touches in this booklet, I am Spartacus. All apply to each of us, but when I thought how one or two might be applicable I relate specifically to Preparation and Persistence. As athletes, both Bill and I know that unless you are dedicated to the regime of preparation that no profession can be excelled in. My ability to win 7 CY Young's in 24 years of professional baseball points to the absolute persistence to the preparation necessary to perform with consistency. Enjoy the read, the principles are unquestionable, as they are true with any professional in the field of athletics, business or music. Preparation and Persistence are the two keys to any professional rising above the competition to excel and be recognized as the champion Gladiator in their field of endeavor.

I AM SPARTACUS....We are all GLADIATORS in our chosen field of endeavor.

There will be four forewords, one from Roger Clemens, 7 times Cy Young Award Winner, 1986 American League MVP and 2 times World Series Champion. Randy Cross, 3 times Super Bowl Champion with the San Francisco 49ers and CBS TV and Radio Celebrity, and Dave Mason, Founder of the rock group Traffic in the mid 1960's and in the Rock and Roll Hall of Fame class, 2004. Dave is a prolific song writer and performer and is currently touring the United States today. Mike Harmon, PGA Professional, Director of Golf at Secession Golf Club and my life long friend since we were 15 years old. Teammate, roommate and life long friend.

A small vignet about the author and things you might see interwoven into the chapters on Goal Setting, Persistence, Preparation, Trust and the 4 Quadrants.

I am fortunate in that I come from a home that was poor, but the teachings of the parents were rich in both moral and religious under pinning's and full of love and giving. On my wife's side of the family is where the sales, marketing and management "family tree" starts to look like a Forest.

My father in law now 83 years old, as of this writing, was a VP of one of the largest outdoor sign companies in America when I started dating his daughter and first met him, in Nashville, Tenn. The stories are voluminous on this mans drive, passion for selling and connections he had cultivated in his work. He was the youngest salesperson ever to be hired by Lever Brothers Company at 20 years old. After 5.5 years he left to join Brach Candy Company and 5 years later was offered a position with a large National Sign company. He worked on commission in order to increase his income to support his ever growing family. He later became Regional Vice President and remained there for 14 years. It was during this time with the sign company that he designed a sign for Colonel Harlan Sanders, owner of Kentucky Fried Chicken The sign was a reproduction of the paper bucket that the Colonel sold full of chicken. The difference was that the illuminated bucket was made from Fiberglass and was lighted inside with fluorescent lights. It became the trademark of each franchise and company store from then on going forward. Colonel Sanders took a liking to Carl and offered him the franchise for Knoxville, Tenn.

Sadly, Carl had to refuse the offer as he did not have the funds necessary to purchase the franchise. Harlan admired Carl's persistence and drive and bought signs continuously from Carl until he sold KFC and retired. When you go to your local drive up teller window at the bank and see the row of silver boxes that light up with a red for closed and a green for open that is because Carl started a company to produce them for banks even before there were automatic teller windows. That was in 1968.

The company continued to grow and Carl sold out to a friend and today it continues as one of the largest bank sign companies in the business. Carl continued to develop companies and retired in 2,000. Now living in the Hilton Head area, he is a treasure chest of stories about persistence and preparation and plain hard work. Nothing replaces preparation, persistence and the enjoyment of doing it for a living. I never heard of anyone dying from hard work.

I am joined in my life's work by my brothers in law, two of which worked with Procter and Gamble directly out of college as did I and the other with Johnson and Johnson. All are highly successful men who have built and sold businesses to Fortune 100 companies and are doing quite well. Here too is a library of knowledge, stories and experiences from which we can continue to recharge our memories of good times. I now enjoy a wealth of knowledge that these professionals have accumulated over the years and am sure they would delight in an opportunity to share them. Wow! What excitement, a reunion of the men in this family ignites when we are all together sharing stories of our careers. Always remember, "Preparation breeds success".

One final story before getting you into the outline and metaphors of Spartacus. When growing up in Atlanta, I would often return to see my Grandmothers (never knew my Grandfathers as they were deceased) who grew up and lived in Augusta, Georgia. My Grandmother, Louise Poole, lived on Washington Road on the same side of the Road as Augusta National and a small 1,000 yard walk to the entry gates. From the time I was 8 until I was 15 my Elementary School and High School teachers would give their permission slips for me to miss Thursday and Friday classes of Masters Week each year. I would be taken to the Greyhound Bus station downtown Atlanta and would make the 20-30 stops along the way on state roads, as there was no I-20 then or they chose not to use the portions that were built. The bus would pull into Augusta late on Wednesday night and my Grandmother and Aunt were there to greet me with that glowing smile of pride and appreciation only we grandparents can impart. So I would walk into the grounds, go the practice tee in front of the clubhouse and watch the greats of Sarazen, Hogan, Nicklaus, Player and my favorite Arnold Palmer. My nickname in high school became Arnie as I led the golf team from my freshman year through senior year. Sorry Mr. Palmer I even started signing annuals at the end of the year "Arnie". More about an Augusta connection some 24 years later…. I was now living in San Francisco and Vice President of Seagram Chateau and Estates Wine Company. We were fortunate to own or represent the best Wine, Champagne, Port businesses in Napa, Monterey, Reims, and Epernay and represent all the best producers of Bordeaux and Burgundy and Alsace.

We had a tour of America happening and one of our brands Champagne Mumm, Reims France, had contracted with the world famous Chef Mr. Paul Bocuse, of Lyon, France. We were doing dinners in varied restaurants all in California at the time and were in Palm Springs, California at the Esmeralda Hotel and dining with Mr. Bocuse, the wine critic from the Los Angeles Times and some local restaurateurs and retailers along with our distributor Southern Wine and Spirits. One of the industry's true "wizards of wine" Mr. Fred Dame, Master Sommelier, who had just joined the company from years of running the famed Sardine Factory wine program in Monterey California. Well Fred went out to the front of the hotel only to run into Mr. Fuzzy Zoeller and asked Fuzzy if he was into playing a joke on a colleague. Anyone who knows Fuzzy understands you just asked him to tee it up and crush it. So Fred reappears in the doorway of this dinner in a private room with all our guests and then I look up and see Fuzzy walk into the room holding a glass of

Orange Juice (Fuzzy Navel). Others recognized the Masters and US Open Champion as well and there was a quick buzz about the room. Fred Dame clinked the glasses to gain attention and hush the crowd. Fuzzy steps forward and asks "Is there some guy in here named Bill Boykin? I want to set up a game with this guy in the morning"... I turned 5 shades of embarrassed red. I sheepishly rose from my chair to go shake Mr. Zoeller's hand and tell him he had found his man. The room erupted with laughter. Well Fuzzy stayed with us partying all night long and at 3 am when we realized we were taking Hot Air Balloons up over the desert floor and then landing to a catered breakfast with Mr. Bocuse, we asked Fuzzy if he wanted to come back in 3 hours and join us. He was the first one in the lobby and called my room to ask where I was....Up I jumped and dressed and got to the lobby for the ride above the desert floor. As Fuzzy learned more about our business, and knew I was a College Golfer and born in Augusta Ga. He said I should call a Mr. Frank Carpenter, head Steward of the Augusta National Golf Club and wine buyer as well. He said the Masters Champion dinners always on Tuesday night of Masters Week would offer wines with the dinner selected by the winner of the tournament the previous year. I did so and Frank and I hit it off. I donated wines several years if the winner did not have their preference and I also became the go to guy for the Bordeaux and Burgundy, Champagne purchases of the Club for many years. Frank is now doing the same services for a prestigious club in Aiken South Carolina. He was a true Gentleman to me and when we went to local Augusta restaurants that were wine destinations he would also break into beautiful songs, as this man could sing like an Opera star. So much more to share about Augusta National, the course, the experiences there but you likely want to get to the meat of the manuscript here.

Chapter 1

THE 4 QUADRANTS OF ASSESSMENT

Understand your surroundings- your opponents and your Teammates

Profiling- one of today's key "buzz words" that the media uses in a politically correct context, to define what someone does, says, thinks or they believe they are thinking that lead to assessing the person you may be focused on. This assessment in today's P.C.S (Politically Correct Society) is again nothing more than judgementalism.

In the REAL WORLD let's use the words assess or assessment in place of Profile or profiling only to be less of a "nerve ending" sensitivity to the polarized left or right that will hopefully read this book.

CHART	SAIL
Use of facts	Forceful Character
Detail Oriented	Persistent
Logic	Leadership
Consistent Performance	Control
Cite Examples	Competitive
Specific Plans Predetermined Manner	Persuasive
KEEL	SIGNAL
Service Oriented	Poised and Sociable
Personal Relationships	Enthusiastic about Causes
Friendly and Empathetic	Praise
Accommodating	Inspired
Use of Suggestions	Personal Contact
	Personal Incentives

Assessment to make tactical decisions #2

THE 4 QUADRANTS	
CHART	SAIL
BE VERSATILE	BE VERSATILE
STRESS PROCESS	STRESS OPTIONS
FEATURE EXPERIENCE	FEATURE RESULTS
KEEL	SIGNAL
BE VERSATILE	BE VERSATILE
STRESS CONCENSUS	STRESS BIG GAINS
FEATURE RELATIONSHIPS	FEATURE NEWEST, LATEST, BEST

THE 4 QUADRANTS			
CHART		**SAIL**	
Details	**How to Handle**	Decisions	**How to Handle**
Process	Bring a PM	Results	Concise
Systems	Show stats	Outcomes	
Methodologies	More Info	Risk OK	Actionable
Background	Give prep time	Challenge OK	
History	No surprises	Business Focus	Be really prepared
		Impatient	Be ready for questions
KEEL		**SIGNAL**	
Friendly	**How to Handle**	Big Picture	**How to Handle**
Social	Reassurance: we'll be there	Vision	
People Oriented		Creativity	Create vision for them
Team Oriented	Easy Going	Get to the Point	Fewer words
Consensus		Subjective	Big idea early
Risk-Averse	Plan Social Activities	Ego-centrism	
Cautious		Emotion	

THE 4 QUADRANTS	
CHART	SAIL
Workspace is activity oriented. Walls May be decorated with diplomas and Other marks of achievement. Office is Organized and work oriented Contact between people is Businesslike.	Efficiency is the theme. Walls may have an appropriate picture or achievement award, but no posters or slogans. Office is activity oriented with a lot of. work materials. Desk may be used for Power positioning
KEEL	SIGNAL
Overall atmosphere is friendly and Open. Look for posters and personal Mementos on walls and desks. Office Is neat and functional. Contact between People is open	General theme is motivation. Walls may be covered with posters and slogans. Atmosphere is friendly and open. Desk may look cluttered and unorganized. Contact between people somewhat open.

Just as the charts made analogies to different traits that put people into these "4 Quadrants of Assessment", it is important for you, The Gladiator, to assess the situation, the person whom you are observing or presenting to. The person's descriptive traits, generally, but of course not always, may give you an idea on positioning statements for your presentation.

As you will see in the book acronyms are used a lot by sales and marketing firms and professional trainers to use as descriptive analysis to basically profile people, which is a sensitive term for many. None the less, it is used by every HR firm in existence to understand the candidates or internally to see how the synergies of the TEAM can be made to be most efficient in this area of diversity.

When you look at the 4 Quadrants they are also oft times compared to the following:

Analytical= Chart
Driver = Keel
Amiable= Sail
Expressive = Signal

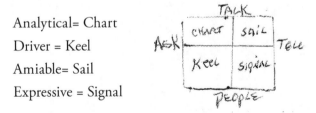

Imagine these in a 4 quadrant box along two axis. Top of the axis = TALK, left side of the equator axis = ASK, to the right of the box along the equator axis = TELL and to the bottom of the box = PEOPLE. When questionnaires are given to assess someone's given tendencies they are plotted or charted along these axis and depending on the higher or lower tendency is where one would plot your dot on the chart. You will land in one or more of these boxes as usually most people have some tendencies in 2 of the quadrants with a primary and secondary tendency. Rarely do you find people with both of their measurement lines with high numbers in the say, Kell or Driver Quadrant. If so, you may be speaking with Attila the Hun.

My point here as it will be later for acronyms is to show there are several similar to almost identical ways in which companies evaluate people and all these trainers in some way have derived this information from the great Consumer goods training grounds, Fortune 500 companies that deliver results.

One person has feel good descriptors as their analogies for the persons they wish to profile and the other group used sailing jargon to describe the same people.

Back to these descriptors: The Charts are made available for you to refer to the attributes and how you might recognize people both in your own company but also within organizations you call on or specific customers you interface with. My purpose in showing these evaluations is to point toward the Preparation segment of any presentation, in that you must first understand and know your opponent or customer as an analogy. Understanding the differences and being able to assess the way to present, the force or lack there of that might be the keys to winning the argument, overcoming the objections and ultimately gaining your POV or sale. These pages will give you a perspective why you and "George from accounting" don't necessarily see eye to eye all the time and are not part of the same weekend football tail gate party.

In life as in business there seems today to be a dividing line of left versus right and a political correctness that has permeated all business culture to the point of sometimes crippling momentum through Human Resources crutched intervention. There will always be the weak people within each culture who you seem to recognize as the ones with that proverbial "rain cloud" following them everywhere. The same people who interject the always destructive conversation ending sex and race cards. Political correctness or this right versus the left attitude has permeated society through a constant barrage of the media shaping most of the populace's opinions as they have become a primary source of our educational base and very few read newspapers anymore and the internet has become a source of blind interpretive criticism that gets uglier and uglier with the all in comments that are allowed through these social mediums.

The press in society and business is the chit chat at the water cooler, the beat of the tom-toms which is the cell phone spread of good news, bad news or gossip…considered truth by some after 15 seconds of airtime. Be aware of people, their strengths, weaknesses and whether you wanted them to have your back in a free for all of Gladiators that on some days is a kill or be killed scenario. Lots of carnage can occur quickly in a company when Trust has deteriorated and there are no functional rules to follow. Ancient Rome conquered most of the known world at the time because their military followed rules and had structure. There were specific fighting teams, the Legions which were 10 groups of 100 led by the Centurion (leader of 100 men). These Legions had allegiance to one Caesar and were governed by one Senate. They had the best clothing, the best weapons, the best training and the best logistics to care for these thousands of men moving from conquest to conquest.

So with the 4 quadrants as a tool for descriptive understanding that there are different personalities, motivations, wants and comfort zones people are motivated to seek or determined to protect. How one maneuvers up and down and across the "silos" of the corporate office or independent office environment is critical to both individual and team success.

Chapter II

GOAL SETTING

If you don't know where you are going you are destined to never arrive

The Gladiator's Goal- Win and Live- STAY ALIVE

The Sales Person's Goal- Make the Sales, achieves the bosses goal, make the commission or salary - STAY ALIVE

The Manager- Focus the sales person, achieves the VP of sales goals given, make the bonus, STAY ALIVE

The COO or CEO, focus the VP of Sales, Marketing, and Finance on the Corporate Goal, appease the Board of Directors, and get the Biggest Bonus, DETERMINE WHO LIVES.

SMAC:

Specific, Measurable, Achievable, Compatible. All your business goals have to be concise and have measures and checks and balances about them for a Goal to really have a tangible lasting result.

Specific: the Goal must be focused and not nebulous. The goal is to grow Brand "X" sales + 15% for the period January – March TY versus same time frame previous year.

Measurable: You have to compare your results to a tangible. It might be build 15 displays in the month of March. Other comparatives are thrown about like KISS- "Keep It Simple Stupid"

Achievable: the only unknown when one starts, as some goals may look simple at first glance and some might appear to be "telephone numbers" A Goal that people give up on before they really get going is useless to set or present. On another scale some don't know how high they can jump until challenged. If the goal is compatible to the boss with the most stripes then that is the goal…

Compatible: The Goal you set individually should be compatible to the Goal of the team, company and corporation you work for.

Interestingly enough as many of us veterans of many corporate jobs and training sessions have seen similar acronyms for what I showed as SMAC. You may also have seen SMART standing for Specific, Measurable, Attainable, Realistic and Timely. Exact same principles with most times the exact same wording as whether your career started out at Procter and Gamble, as mine did, or you came from Gallo Wines (large P&G Fraternity), Johnson and Johnson, Coca-Cola etc almost all, NO EXACTLY ALL of them use some derivative of SMAC.

> Again, you will find a myriad of acronyms used by sales teachers, almost all derived from the same key consumer goods companies that gave you the SMAC acronym, For the 5 steps of The Presentation you may see the O.P.E.R.A. acronym.
>
> Overview of the Situation
> Propose the Idea
> Explain how it works
> Reinforce key benefits
> Ask for the order
>
> As you can see they are exactly alike in everyway but an added word here or sentence to just say CLOSE? The message

is clear, use the 5 steps of the presentation as they are necessary and fool proof.

Step 4 in reinforcing the key benefits needs a little more attention as it is here that the buyer interjects their objections. These can be real or false, however both must be attended to with forthright answers and to the point.

Here are some more acronyms to remember as it applies to the Objection Process:

S.A.C.K

Show you understand fully, the objection

Answer candidly. Deal with the buyer's concern and repeat one of the key benefits from point number 4.

Check with the buyer for their satisfaction in your answering their concerns (objection)

Keep moving forward to closure. Return to your step 5 and close the sale. If another objection arises you answer it candidly, ask for buyer understanding and satisfaction and then return to the close.

See the chart about buyer personalities and remember the 4 quadrants as these traits are derived directly by personality traits/styles of the person you are now trying to sell.

PERSONALITY STYLES

FIGHT	FLIGHT
Complainer	**Silent**
• Show empathy • Listen patiently • Restate with Benefits • Demonstrate Profitability	• Listen carefully • Encourage with questions • Don't dominate • Allow silence
Expert	**Agreeable**
• Acknowledge expertise • Don't be defensive • Seek their advice • Give them credit	• Raise the concern • Validate the concern • Confirm the solution • Restate and validate
Aggressor	**Indecisive**
• Allow venting • Stay fact focused • Clarify the complaint • Solve the problem	• Build trust • Provide "best" solution • Use small closes • Reaffirm decision

Chapter III

PREPARATION: PHYSICAL, MENTAL, FACT FINDING, LAY-OUT, TIME UTILIZATION

Just like any Gladiator, you must stay in shape. Jog, Run, Walk, Lift, but do some Physical exercise to stay focused and fit enough to withstand the rigors of travel, stress and bad dietary or life decisions we all seem to make.

Work the hours, work smart and forget the clock

No short cuts, reports- fill them out; fill them out on time and completely, accurately

Be the Early worm- Lombardi time; never be late to a meeting, a presentation, any function. Tardiness is first a show of disrespect to all who were called to and agreed to a specific meeting time. Show up 20 minutes late to an NFL game and it is deep into the second quarter.

Back your boss- even the scriptures say we must follow the rules set forth by the rulers and those edicts are sometimes hard to follow and accept. Until the boss breaks the law, tells an untruth about you that is blatant and meant to cause you pain, and even then it is your job to make the boss or Gladiator owner/trainer look good.

Be prepared to leave your Gladiator camp (Headhunters are there for a reason) and seek a new opportunity or a new boss if there is mistreatment. Not everyone is your mom or dad and wishes the best for you.

Understand others that are weak, take short cuts or are "Children of Caesar" get positions they don't deserve, can't perform and many will try and take you down. Most often due to jealousy or paranoia. You will experience these weak, shallow and untalented people. DO NOT BE SURPRISED-DO NOT DISPAIR. Be forewarned other Gladiators will scheme against you. You will no doubt get nicked up, injured and maybe spill a little blood (an analogy people) but the key is to stay alive. Spartacus must fight again tomorrow and so must you to make tomorrows calls tomorrows meeting.

You will see attacks based on sexism, racism, your cultural background or past socio-economic upbringing as a means of positioning you for a lower rung on the ladder or to hurt you in terms of an HR issue falsely created.

Keep good journals about every experience so when you are challenged, and it will happen in life, you have a close to verbatim description of the conversations, or verbal degradations you might suffer. As long as your integrity and morality are intact you will beat back the people who feel entitled and who wish to cause you problems as they generally do not have enough on the ball to win the real argument or battle inside the business arena. Realize some of these are created and driven by narcissists. Sometimes you just have to bow, retreat and live to fight another day.

In Gladiatorial matches there was always a referee standing next to the two combatants. Unfortunately in life this Referee may be called Human Resources and not always on your side as many times there seems to be a hidden agenda. The best HR directors are awesome as they are enforcers who must also guide, provide most of the training exercises within a company and be a sounding board for hearing disputes and in most cases diffusing these employee concerns before it even becomes a face to face encounter with a superior which in most cases does not work well for the disgruntled employee.

Preparation, persistence, integrity, study, knowledge, dressing for success and political savvy are all tools and attributes one must possess to be a successful Gladiator in the sales arena.

Gladiators were the WWF, professional athletes, and sports stars of their time. They were 95% slaves (yes you too are an indentured servant to the corporate entity you work for) The owners (senior management) pampered and made sure their best Gladiators (producers) received the best training, the best amour, the best weapons for his or her skill set, even companionship was offered to keep the libido in check. Matched pairs had referees standing next to the combatants as not all matches were matches "to the death". In fact, most matches were for show. These Gladiators were expensive to groom, train, produce and these "games" which is a metaphor for tickets to today's sports spectacles and produced revenue for the Gladiator's owner. Thus the sales person of today who is strong, dresses well, produces above and beyond the Goals given becomes pampered much like the Gladiators of old.

Unfortunately for us all, we age. Gladiators aged as well, which was not a desired thing in the Ancient times as the older Gladiator would be "offered up" for death matches where one of the combatants surely perished.

Key is stay in shape, physically and mentally. Train hard on all aspects of the job requirement and assignment. Produce wins and ultimately win the freedom from Caesar with the granting of either the rudius, false sword of freedom, or be allowed to exit the arena graciously and gracefully. Like any who are lucky enough to retire, Spartacus had dreams of that village along the Coast …

Another real life story for you in terms of Preparation:

It is 7:30 am in the morning and your phone rings at home and your immediate supervisor or boss is on the line and says to meet him in an hour at 8:30 at the coffee shop you both frequent close to your home.

This is a true story about real events that were common place at Procter and Gamble any of their sales divisions when they had direct sales forces.

1. Assumption for you here is that this is 1977 and that the company assumed you would be walking out by 8 am to head for your first accounts for the day. Expectation is most reps would hit 8-12 accounts a day depending on shelving or display work required in the day's accounts.
2. If you as the representative were not prepared for that days sales calls, meaning that you had prepared the night before all visuals and mathematics needed for that day and also had not prepared your sales reports for mailing then the review would not go well.

The point here is if you were not prepared and all work had not been completed in its entirety and completely then this

"Surprise review or Curbstone Conference" would separate the real producers from the pretenders.

Be Prepared as you never know when your "Curbstone Conference" will be called.

Be Prepared:

1. Your presentation will be better
2. Your client/customer/distributor appreciates the efforts
3. Results = $
4. Continuous Results + $$$ and potential Promotions $$$$

There are many ways to describe the preparation and pattern the successful sales associate uses whether they are walking in a store to sell alcoholic beverages, or a clothing representative walking into a store to make a presentation on a new clothing line or a financial consultant walking into an office situation to make a cold call on a banker, or record producer's office or some coaches office in the NFL or Professional baseball owner/manager's office complex.

Here are some guide lines to refer to:

1. Prepare to make the call (do your research ahead of time, lay-out the presentation on paper in advance)

2. Enter the account or office complex like a professional- DRESS FOR SUCCESS

3. Survey the account for obvious opportunities or to size up the interests of the person to be seen (picture/plaques on the wall, award plaques, sports, theater or children interests)

4. If it is retail then work the shelving /displays and be aware of competitive action

5. Make the Presentation: remember the 5 steps of the presentation.- always follow the 5 steps.

6. Thank the account /buyer/person to be seen for their time, their business, their consideration, their order.

7. Wrap up the call, visit and move to your next call, your next interview, your next conquest.

Chapter IV

THE 5 STEPS OF THE PRESENTATION

Although a short chapter because the steps are but 5, the principles are interconnected to your preparation and your persistence, but the fundamentals of the Presentation are enduring, simple yet powerful when repeated and memorized as to why their order is so critical.

1. Summarize the Situation: In a generalization you focus the buyer or person you are pitching of the idea to follow; "If I could show you a way to maximize your expenditures and increase your business in October 20% would you be interested? Who isn't going to say yes to that summation?

2. State the Idea Clearly- 'I would like to put a display of "X" on the end of aisle 5 to tie in with our TV ad and return you $$.

3. Explain how it works- Show them the math of the profit per case on the number of cases you

want them to buy. Why the end of aisle 5 and the particulars of why this deal is right for them

4. Re-enforce the key benefits. This is the section where the objections may arise. You handle the objection, answer the objection. If it is a false objection, that gets tossed out but if real you must address either their disbelief of your numbers or some element of your Idea or the situation. Once you have answered the objection and reached agreement by saying "Did that adequately answer your question?" Great--- then you immediately move to close

5. The Close- did you want that delivered on Tuesday or Wednesday? Several methods of closing from assumptive close to asking them a question about delivery dates.

Although this chapter could simply be The 5 Steps of the Presentation with very little explanation, there is one of the steps that can and does take the most time to conquer. All your oratory skills and thinking quick on your feet with a recall for your earlier words, facts and figures is mandatory.

Step#4 Re- enforce the Key Benefits

Imagine if you will that you have summarized the holiday selling situation brilliantly. Your succinct Idea was spot on. You then explained the mathematics of your idea, how it benefitted the buyer both in top line sales but bottom line profits based on his consumers buying habits and tendancies. You then move to Re-enforce these Key Benefits.

Re-enforce Key Benefits can also be described as the gate keeper to the close. You reiterate the benefits in a summation of your previously explained facts in the explain how it works section. The buyer by stopping you to ask a question or interject a direct opinion is throwing their first OBJECTION.

If and when, as they most often all object to some point or time of delivery. Make sure you Recognize Clearly and Respectfully that you indeed heard their objection.

1. You re-state the objection –sometimes when your mirror the objection back to them they realize how trivial it might be and say I got it and lets move on.
2. Answer the objection using the facts you presented or inject further data if the objection requires an add on to what you already presented.
3. Once you have answered the objection or concern, then get an agreement of Satisfaction. The customer is happy with your covering the objection and you may then move directly to The Close.

How to handle personality styles

Chart	How to handle	Sail	How to handle
Details	Bring a PM	Decisions	Concise
Process	Show stats	Results	Actionable
Systems	More info	Outcomes	Be really prepared
Methodologies	Give prep time	Risk OK	Be ready for
Background	No surprises	Challenge OK	questions
History		Business Focus	
		Impatient	
Keel	**How to handle**	**Signal**	**How to handle**
Friendly	Reassurance: we'll	Big Picture	Create vision
Social	be there	Vision	for them
People oriented	Easy-going	Creativity	Fewer words
Team oriented	Plan social activities	Get to the point	Big idea early
Consensus		Subjective	
Risk-averse		Ego-centrism	
Cautious		Emotion	

See the chart of people's personality styles, here. Remember the 4 quadrants. See some similarities in the two charts? In the south we use many colloquialisms or expressions to inject humor or make a point without insulting someone. It is all about the delivery, voice inflection, facial smiling, hand gestures and body language.

In the case where both parties have agreed to the problem being identified you might here a saying like: "If it walks like a Duck, and quacks like a Duck, it just might be a freaking Duck.

Once or twice in the South I have heard buyers say, when disparaging a sales associates mental capacity to perform a certain job requested by said buyer… "That guy could not pour water (or some expletive) from a boot with directions written on the heel". Or the buyer agreeing that a product is likely to sell well in a particular store location.. "That dog will hunt" and finally when the buyer throws this killer objection more than once you may want to pull out product number two. This classic.. "The dogs are not eating the dog food", might be handled on objection number one, but if he throws that at you twice, you likely are on to product presentation number 2.

If your customer or buyer allows you to go through your re-enforcing the key benefits without interruption or Objection then you immediately transition to: THE CLOSE

> Always follow the same pattern of setting up the situation, stating the idea clearly, and then explain how it all works and that it benefits them to say yes. The fourth step is where objections go to die. If they arise, they are handled then you return immediately to step 5. You don't talk it to death. DO NOT RE-THINK THE IDEA. TOO MANY LOOSE LIPS SINK SHIPS. The close – you did your proper preparation, you had the store or arena mapped out and knew the math by Memory. You could make this sale in your sleep- Why? YOU ARE SPARTACUS...

Chapter V

PERSISTENCE

The summer of 1976, Southwestern Book Company is the setting and the employer for the summer vacation turned to workaholics anonymous, the summer of persistence.

Have you ever had 20-30 front doors of houses slammed in your face, each day, and 6 days a week for 10 straight weeks? That was my experience the summer of 1976 as a Sigma Chi Fraternity brother recruited me to sell books door to door the summer before my senior year at Middle Tenn. State University.

The company, who recruits college students to canvass and sell their products door to door nationwide, a kind of Fuller Brush salesman attack, on steroids. The company located in Nashville, Tenn. would have all the recruits come to an inexpensive hotel close by their sprawling campus for a week of training. Primarily motivational speakers and examples of what you might encounter on this strange but incredible journey you were to embark on... Most importantly they taught you how to walk up to a home, smile, give them a line or two about their neighbors, with their real names and wipe your feet, asking permission to enter their home and you were inside. They also gave you several situational selling skits to prepare you, somewhat for what you were about to encounter. I started to feel like the guy in Close Encounters of the Third Kind at this point.

I was assigned the Chambersburg, Pennsylvania town to settle into, find a place to rent and use as my hub for working these 10 weeks. You were given a Rand McNally road map (No GPS or cell phones in 1976) and using this detailed map you would set out each day like a spoke on a wheel going down every street, every lane, country road in a radius that would take you deeper and farther from the home base. Mine took me deep into Amish country and near enough to Gettysburg to travel there on Sunday's to soak in the history.

The product line I had to sell was:

1. The Big Home Family Bible- every coffee table needed one
2. The Naves Topical Bible- excellent book laid out like a dictionary where you find verses –all of them that are on a topic. Look up cats and it would list

every verse in the bible that mentioned or dealt with cats.

3. Home Medical Journal- every home needed a medical reference book in case of emergencies

4. Children Book series. 4 plastic coated page books that were for the 2-6 range.

I had something for everyone. If there were a Big Family Bible sitting on that coffee table I went to book number two, if that failed then on to Medical book, and if no children were present I would work them for names of the neighbors both next door and across the street for my next cold call and the next adventure in selling.

Armed with a small square green box with a lock latch on the front, which contained samples of all the books I might present. Once I had entered the house I would look for the best seat in the house and lead the person to that spot, his chair or if a woman you would say where would you like to sit "madam" I am a southerner and with my southern drawl in Pennsylvania I was easy to spot as not being from the area. Once they sat down I would open the box, spread the books in front of them like jewels and close the box and sit directly at their feet on that box. It was holding my tools and was my footstool all in one.

Some of these sales calls include calling on farmers while in their barns milking cows. Presenting to farmers on their tractors. In Amish country, you would present to a farmer hooked up to horses and plow. Also in Amish country I presented to families by candlelight as in some sects of this religious group electricity was banned from the house. Much of the ways in which the people lived seemed to be right out of the 1600-1700's..

In the end, there were some 1,800-1,900 houses and farms I had called on. I then in week 11 went back along the same routes to deliver each of these sold books. I had collected 50% of the books cost when I first met them all cash or check. When I returned if they did not want the books I kept the 50% and returned the book to the company for a credit to my account. At the end of the deliveries you immediately, as fast as my silver and racing stripe black Vega would take me return to Nashville. First though a stop to see my future wife to be Diane Montgomery, in Knoxville as I drove south from Pennsylvania. The next morning I would leave to Nashville for the cash out. You checked into a line at the warehouse. You unloaded on a roller, if necessary the books you were returning and they were rung up as credits to all you had ordered. Next you gave them all the cash and checks you brought with you from the last days of collecting as you made deposits everyday, as their were vast sums of money each day and you remitted from the bank daily to your account in Nashville. Well, they counted all the cash, deducted the net amount owed for the books and cut you a final check for what you had earned NET for the entire summers work. My check was over $3,000. This is after I paid my rent, my food, my gasoline and any incidental cash I spent while out for these 11 weeks. Not sure how the reader will perceive this story but to have any college student save any money from their summer job let alone $3,000 was a solid accomplishment.

I also received a special award for working 80 hours a week for the full 10 weeks. That was hitting your first door at 8 and leaving your last house at 8 pm each day for 6 days and 10 weeks. Not counting your driving time to the first account and home that night. Closer to 6 am to 9 pm.

Persistence Meeting Exercise

The Ten Balloons:

Visualize the speakers stage has ten helium filled balloons arranged horizontally across the stage. They are about 8 feet in the air for me as it needs to have effect. (At 6 foot 3 and a wing span to almost 8 feet you will see this effect)

The speaker tells his audience that today's message is all about perseverance. Make the calls, no short cuts and you will see results, build account rapport and respect and start your climb to the title of Sales Expert.

Standing in front of the first balloon the speaker starts describing an account by name everyone in that audience would likely know or at least be familiar with. He says the sales associate walks in the front door and waves at the buyer as he is approaching and says, "Do you need anything today". I reach up and pop the balloon. The noise wakes up the normal meeting sleep walkers and I just stare for a moment at several in the room. Silence is a great tool to use to bring focus back to any conversation. I say terrible just terrible. I move to balloon number 2 and set it up with an account name. I then describe the sales associate walking in and saying hello and telling them he wants to walk the store and take care of his section and will get with them in a moment on some great new deals. He /she then proceeds to walk the store perimeter looking for possible display locations, cross merchandising locations. The associate then goes to the shelf and sees what might be different with the set, new items from competitors, and then pulls up and straightens what they are allowed to do. If there is a display/s the associate goes to pull up the empties and consolidate so they can ask for more products to replenish. Armed with knowledge of the store, the fact they have done their good deed with shelving and display clean up they have an arsenal of additional things to include in their presentation.. Remember those 5 steps of the presentation? The associate sets the situation, states clearly the idea, shows the buyer the math on paper already prepared, readies for re-enforcing the key benefits and any objections that might be brought up and then closes. It happens like that in succession on each call. GREAT CALL THIS BALLOON STAYS IN THE AIR AS A SALUTE TO EXCELLENCE

The presentation by the presenter moves down the stage with 8 more stories about accounts they know, buyers they know and at the end there are 4 Balloons left in the air.

The presenter starts with a melancholy wow there are just 4 balloons out of ten left and hangs their head for a moment in silence. Then springs exuberantly to life and says you know what this means. This person who had 10 calls and made them all, some good and some not so good is still batting 400. You bat 400 for your career and you are in the sales

Hall of Fame. And you have become SPARTACUS. You won, you won all the time and you were PERSISTENT.

Several things are at play here from earlier chapters. You had to use knowledge of the 4 Quadrants to read the buyer. You had to prepare for the calls and those you did the best preparation for are the ones you usually sold. You had to be persistent as there are interruptions and traffic and calls you receive. However, you made sure you saw all 10 calls because you had made your goal and you stuck to that target. You then made your Presentation utilizing the 5 steps procedure. So you might see how these start to be intertwined into the fabric of building sales excellence. This could apply to the CFO and dealing with 10 invoices that day or talking to ten sources of finance for money needed for liquidity. The Marketing VP has ten meetings to determine ads or POS for the brands and the brand managers that need to be seen to make that happen. It applies to the Insurance salesman, the car salesman, or the phone canvasser. Make the 10 calls happen and do it consistently and you will become good at your chosen vocation or profession.

Chapter VI

TRUST

In previous companies I would send emails to my direct reports where I use analogies about Spartacus and to thank them for their efforts and also ask for their guidance in making me a better person, a better man, and better leader. You hope those you are assigned to hire, then train, then lead, find time to look for the wisdom you are trying to impart. As gamesmanship does tend to rear its ugly head from time to time I try and give abstract examples to draw correlations to the actual jobs we perform, people we interact with and survival within our own job, our own company and our own circumstances.

A few quotes on TRUST:

Colin Powell once said "Why would you follow anyone around a corner? Or up a hill? Or into a dark room? The reason is TRUST"

"Trust is the key moral of our times" James Burke, former CEO of Johnson and Johnson

"I know only that moral is what you feel good after and immoral is what you feel bad after" Ernest Hemingway

"A man is already of consequence in the world when it is known that we can implicitly rely upon him. Often I have known a man to be preferred in stations of honor and profit because he had the reputation: when he said he knew a thing, he knew it, and when he said he would do a thing, he did it" Edward Bulwer-Lytton

You can rest assured Spartacus dealt with the term TRUST. He had to trust his owners, his trainers, his weapons, and his physical strength to get him through matched pairs. He had to trust his fellow Gladiators when they planned and executed their rebellion against Rome. His men trusted him to the point where they were willing to say they were "SPARTACUS" when the Romans had defeated them and corralled them after a disastrous battle. These men were all yelling 'I am Spartacus" knowing full well that the punishment was to be immediately crucified and still they loved and trusted their leader enough to make that sacrifice. Later in history, my lord and savior, Jesus Christ would say "There is no greater love than for a man to lay down his life for his friends".

The Trust Meeting:

In a sales meeting or meeting of executives, it is usually best or advised to do this exercise with a senior group of executives who hopefully have worked together for some time. Harder with a big room filled with all levels of business maturity as this exercise will test that maturity both mentally and physically and emotionally.

The Moderator, let's say that is Spartacus for this illustration, at the podium and he has delivered several stories about different elements of the QUADRANT or Preparation or Goal Setting which has relaxed or bored his audience to a point where this exercise will wake them up and for some, scare them to death.

I will ask all the executives to stand up, clear the chairs and desks to the side of the room so we have an empty space or you can move to an adjacent empty room for this exercise. By removing the chairs and desks you have removed a crutch or hiding spot. Standing in the midst of their peer group is a nerve racking affair for many.

I then ask the participants to look about the room and pair up. Get with a person you want to start this exercise with. The quick minds and schemers now think I will get with my closest ally for this exercise and we will conquer. The strategy of war has already started. Remember the quadrant as you will see the differences in play among this diverse group..

Spartacus now says to the group for each of the pairs to stand facing each other so close that the toes of their shoes are touching, if physiques allow. Once you are in someone's "space" and feel their breaths you are at a totally different place. Most of these executives manage from afar.

Spartacus now bursts their initial planning/scheming bubble with the rules of engagement for this entire exercise:

1. This is a TRUST exercise
2. You will be pairing off with every person in this room for the duration of this exercise whether it be the President, your boss or head of Finance you will pair up just as you are now in each others space
3. Here are the instructions as you face your partner in this death match
4. You must look into the eyes of the person you are so close to, not look away but directly into their eyes and tell them that on a scale of 1 to 10, I trust you "X" and then immediately what it would take that person doing to get that rating to a 10.
5. Now you must tell the person why you distrust them or why the rating is the way it is
6. The other person in this pair must repeat the steps in #4 and 5

With the instructions given in number 4, some have now had their mind shift to the person they have issues with or don't really know in the room. They thought they were going to beat the system, beat this exercise by picking their best ally. Well, Spartacus just threw them into the Arena and today the lions are hungry.

I can tell you from experience I have been a participant in this exercise and it obviously made a lasting impression on me to find its way into this book. It is difficult because you have 2 minutes per person to do your explanation. The answers or explanation are often times gut wrenching..

Spartacus then asks all the participants to pull the chairs and desks into the meeting room formation prior to the exercise beginning.

1. How did it initially feel to hear the instructions to pair up?
2. Did you gravitate toward a friend/colleague of TRUST value?
3. When you heard you would be repeating this exercise with every person in the room where did your mind roam?
4. How did it feel to be rated on the 1 to 10 scale?

Remember that you were inches apart and telling someone rapidly on a grading scale (we all hate small numbers or an A-F grade scale of us). As it occurs you are fully in shock, hurt, in disarray, stunned eyes of hurt despair and even squinting anger may possess you at the moment of the first sword strike. This is the factual dealings of building a TEAM. In a group of diversified talents they need to better understand their strengths or weaknesses and where the TRUST factors are. They can then shore up these holes of mistrust and when called upon be there to help, assist and cheer for the Gladiator in the Arena. We, who are about to Die, Salute You. Some of your team dies every day in the sales call arena. Not all calls are successful. The marketplace is competitive. There is always a bigger, more fierce Gladiator in the next town to face and do battle with. Imagine you are the chosen Gladiator for the battle in the arena that day. You are given your matched pair assignment just moments before the doors swing open and the bloody sands of the arena floor and your opponent are now fully visible. You must move forward to accept the challenges of this battle to the death. You are given your weapons by the referee for this fight and on this day you are given your choice. You pick the cell phone and brief case. (Work with me here)

You immediately dial the home office to get some data on your opponent, only to get a recording that they will get back to you? You immediately dial your boss, who says abruptly, I am busy, handle it and hangs up. The referee steps forward removes your cell phone, as there was a two call maximum. I know you may be saying, "But I did not know that war and business have rules?" What rules, there are no rules!

The Gladiator now reaches down to his trusted brief case to find it empty as the Gladiator had watched the wrestling matches the night before and had not prepared any data for fighting this opponent. The Gladiator is now at the sales call facing the buyer, opponent, with no back up, no data and no support team.

It did not go well for the unprepared and unsupported Gladiator. Can you draw similar parallels to your daily existence, your fights/sales calls? I use sales as the metaphor for Gladiator but it is the same with Marketing, Finance or any other department in the corporate environment. You see, we must all answer to someone. We all have our "matched pairs". We all yearn for a TEAM that you have confidence in, that has your back and will support you in your efforts to help the TEAM succeed.

Well, let's try this exercise in your company and see where the TRUST factor is. If you get your entire team to where they rank each other as a 7-8 across the board you will beat any competitor. Your company will be "politically" healthier and a sense of well being will be derived by all members of the TEAM. Those suppliers, distributors, and customers you interact with will feel it and sense it as well when they see your TEAM in action.

Spartacus addresses his army of Gladiators:

SPARTACUS AND HERMANN IN THE ARENA.

Some may say, reading this only applies to the sales guys. It applies to every person within their own departments. If you want to be CFO, the odds are you had to do well in math classes early in life, that you were proficient with spread sheets, statistical analysis, economics and many other courses to prepare you mentally for what you think is a fun profession. Remember the 4 QUADRANTS. If the sales "Gladiator" were to have the same interests, drive, and long terms goals as the back room administrator then not much would happen in that company or group. People are driven differently because there are the differences in what drives people to succeed. Some in life like stability, no travel, pay checks on time, insurance for the family and all those things combined spell security to that person. Some are driven by ambition to either rule the sales, marketing or finance world and they go about their daily preparation and goal setting differently from support staffs.

So whether you are selling an insurance policy or selling the CEO on releasing funds to buy longer stores of raw materials for future growth you expect on the horizon, the principles of how you make that presentation are always the same. Stay consistent and when you structure literally thousands of presentations over a career you have what head hunters call EXPERIENCE. Spartacus called it experience as well because he prepared and followed the same clear principles of understanding his situation and then using his strength, skills and drives to stay alive and win.

If I do a talk for your company or group I will interject the many different people, celebrities, sports and music stars that are part of my life's experiences. I have run sales divisions, run companies, owned companies and been on Boards. The same things that I wrote about in the preceding chapters on SMAC, KISS, the 5 steps of the presentation, the preparation tasks necessary, and the 4 quadrants allow me to use group participation to add clarity.

Remember again in the arena of Ancient Rome, the Gladiators turned to Caesar and said in unison, "We who are about to die salute you". Life is a tough and sometimes unforgiving place. Ego and false witness have destroyed many a company. One must trust in management to have the well being of their entire roster of employees and provide the training tools, and the TRUST in them to perform their jobs with excellence.

Life is a series of days in which you as the Gladiator must get up and hopefully thank God for your many blessings. Assume you will enter and exit the arena as a winner. It means that you prepared well, you set your Goal finitely, your presentation was tight and on point for the 5 steps and you were able to do so because your support staff instilled confidence and a sense of Trust that someone had your back.

I have been both a Gladiator and Caesar. I can tell you from experience that both are difficult professions. Both are best off and remembered best like Spartacus and Julius Caesar. Both men were strong willed, strong physically (although Julius Caesar did suffer a form of epilepsy). Both men prepared better, were stronger, supported by their followers and enjoyed the best weapons, advice, logistics and strategy. There were literally millions of Gladiators who gave their lives for the perverted enjoyment of the masses and yet we remember SPARTACUS as the Gladiator who rebelled and fought against the tyranny of slavery which was Rome. He was defeated and in the end was crucified by the orders of a then, Centurion named Julius Caesar, as his commander so ordered him to do. Julius Caesar's accomplishments are many from Egypt to Gaul and in the end he was assassinated by friends and the Senate who were supposed to be his supreme support staff. Those that were part of the plot did not fair well afterwards, as the loyalty of the Army which he led hunted down and killed those who had killed him.

Today's society mirrors much of what we saw in ancient Rome. In today's society we seem consumed with the right or left. Rome was a powerful society with a strong military and a Senatorial government with Governors or prefects to provide entertainment, food subsidies and protection to the masses. Rome too became fractured, lost its moral compass and through a succession of very strange, twisted and corrupt people from Caligula to Nero, decayed rapidly from within. In between were, good Caesars such as Marcus Aurelius but in the system of nepotism and in breeding we get Commodus the son? Such was the chaos that was Rome and that Gladiator had to live and perform within it.

Now back to killing it like SPARTACUS. Prepare better, support better, love your family better, protect the helpless and give relentlessly.

From the perspective of Spartacus he too would follow the guidelines we have espoused in this book.

1. Understand your opponent- the 4 Quadrant principles
2. Set your Goal definitively- SMAC
3. Preparedness on all levels is key
4. Persistence is a determination to succeed
5. Trust is the backbone of a organization small or large.

My favorite saying is "It does not cost a penny extra to be nice". I hope the Golden Rule is your measuring stick in life. I wish you every success you want. It is there for you to take, win your fights in life, and be the next SPARTACUS.

Boss	Leader
Drives employees	Coaches them
Depends on authority	On goodwill
Inspires Fear	Generates enthusiasm
Says "I"	Says "We"
Places Blame for breakdown	Fixes the breakdown
Knows how it is done	Shows how it is done
Uses People	Develops people
Takes Credit	Gives Credit
Commands	Asks
Says "Go"	Says "Let's go"

ABOUT THE AUTHOR

The author has spent the past 4 decades in sales, sales management, an entreprenurial owner and at no time since the age of 25 has he had a business title less than Vice President in any company for whom he was employed. That adds up to a lot of EXPERIENCE.

Printed in the United States
By Bookmasters